D1015627

Confessions
of an Unbalanced
Woman

Confessions of an Unbalanced Woman

EMILY WATTS

DESERET
BOOK

SALT LAKE CITY, UTAH

Visit us at deseretbook.com

Library of Congress Cataloging-in-Publication Data
Watts, Emily.
    Confessions of an unbalanced woman / Emily Watts.
        p.   cm.
    ISBN 1-59038-587-X (hardbound : alk. paper)
    1. Mormon women—Religious life.   2. Christian life—Mormon authors.   3. Christian life—Humor.   I. Title.
    BX8641.W38 2006
    248.8′43—dc22
                                                            2006007338

Printed in Mexico
R.R. Donnelley and Sons, Reynosa, Mexico

10   9   8   7   6   5

Confessions of an Unbalanced Woman

I THINK I FIRST RECOGNIZED the lack of balance in my life over a pile of socks. Socks were not a new phenomenon in my life—I have a husband and five children—but on that particular day they seemed especially puzzling. I don't know how it is that I can spend hours laboring over a stack of men's socks, laying them out on the bed to make it easier to compare them with each other, holding them up to the light, even carry-ing them over to the window to ensure that I am matching black with black and navy blue with navy blue . . . but the instant my husband sits down in sacrament meeting, I can tell that he's wearing one of each. Maybe there's just something about the lighting in the chapel. Maybe I should be taking his socks over to the church to sort them.

I have three sons, and so I've spent another good chunk of my life trying to keep their socks straight. The style when my kids were small was for boys' socks to have colored stripes around the top; therefore, I always had a huge basket full of strays: one red stripe, two blue stripes, a company logo. Then I read a hint in a women's magazine: Buy the same plain white tube socks for all your boys and you'll never have more than one left-over in any given batch of laundry. I went right to the store and picked up thirty-six pairs of identical tube socks.

After a couple of weeks, though, I realized that I couldn't bear to make the meticulous child wear the same socks as the kid with the kind of stinky feet who didn't really change his socks often enough anyway. Soon I found myself matching those socks *by gray-scale*. This is no way to live a balanced life.

I knew the madness had to stop, but it was actually my husband who pointed out the obvious solution to me. He looked me gently in the eyes and said, "You know, honey, these kids are perfectly capable of doing their own laundry." I'm embarrassed to admit that this had not even occurred to me. I was the mom, and I had always operated under the assumption that doing the laundry was the mom's job. And that was probably true when the children were four and two years old, but now that they were fourteen

I was the mom, and I had always operated under the assumption that doing the laundry was the mom's job.

and twelve, and had several more siblings, it wasn't working so well. I quickly developed a new philosophy: "Wash a kid a sock, and you clothe him for a day . . ." I don't even have to finish that thought, do I?

So now we teach our kids to do laundry at quite a tender age. We always start them out with the towels, because towels are fairly forgiving. If you get the light ones in with the dark ones, it's not usually that big a deal. More important, towels have no pockets in which to hide Chapstick or brown crayons or half-bags of Skittles or other perfectly innocuous items that become deadly only when they hit the inside of a dryer.

One day when one of the children was running a load of towels, I was working in the kitchen when I heard a terrible noise in the laundry room. I rushed downstairs to find my washing machine rocking and groaning like a wounded animal. Hurrying to lift the lid and stop the cycle, I looked into the machine to see what might be wrong. It turned out there was no space in that machine in which there was not a towel. I started to pry the wet towels out, which is not such an easy task even when the machine is not overloaded. I have a large-capacity washing machine, and I need it. But it was not meant to hold fourteen, full-size bath towels. However, the kids labor under the illusion (and sometimes even their father espouses this belief) that if you can cram it into the machine, and the lid closes, you can wash the load.

The kids labor under the illusion that if you can cram it into the machine, and the lid closes, you can wash the load.

Well, if you consistently wash fourteen towels in a machine that was designed to hold ten, what will happen? You will break your machine! Maybe not the first time, or the second, but ultimately. In fact, when the washer is rocking and groaning in the manner I have described, there's a term for it—they say the machine is "out of balance." That seems almost eerily appropriate.

Anyway, from this experience with the laundry I have derived a metaphor for my whole existence: I am a fourteen-towel woman in a ten-towel-capacity life. No wonder I feel so out of balance! I have lots to do, and all of it is good and worthwhile and important, but I simply can't do it all at once. How can I balance every-thing? This became the object of a serious quest for me.

Plan A:
Time Management

I BEGAN MY SEARCH FOR balance by attending a time-management seminar. At this enlightening event, I learned how to plan carefully and how to make a list and prioritize it so the most important things would get done first. It helped—for a little while. But then would come the kind of day (and this happens more often than you would believe) when everything falls apart.

You know these days. A child comes home from school on the verge of tears. He finally manages to confess that he has a science project due—tomorrow. This is a term project. He got the assignment outline six weeks ago. It has resided in the bottom of his backpack since that day. All right, there will be time for discussion and recriminations and regrets later on. For now, we must rally to the cause. We smooth out the paper together to learn what must be done.

There will be time for discussion and recriminations and regrets later on. For now, we must rally to the cause.

The assignment is to make a model of a cell. I leave the child in the kitchen rummaging around in the backs of the cupboards for things like split peas and dry macaroni to represent mitochondria and ribosomes and vacuoles and the other parts of the cell, while I dash off to the craft store for a half-sphere of Styrofoam (which I never seem to have lying about the house when needed). When I get back, the child has moved on to the toy chest in search of an old golf ball with which to create a suitable nucleus, and I spend the next half-hour with a serrated knife trying to saw a ball of Styrofoam in half because they didn't *have* a half-sphere at the craft store. Little bits of foam are floating everywhere in the air, but we're making some progress. Husband and other children have been sent out for pizza long since, so the decks are clear in that regard.

Soon the child retires to the computer to type up the labels for the cell parts, and I fire up the glue gun. If OSHA made home inspections, I am convinced I would be forbidden to use a glue gun. I have no skill in this arena. Just about all I can do with hot glue is string it in long strands all over the work area and burn my fingers. But there is no other way that I know of to adhere a split pea to a Styrofoam surface, so I make the sacrifice.

> If OSHA made home inspections, I am convinced I would be forbidden to use a glue gun.

It is very late by the time I get everything glued on and the child finishes the labels and the accompanying report for the cell, but the project *is* finished at last, and we stagger off to bed. The next morning, I drop the child and the cell off at school and return home to find the playroom strewn with every piece of every old, abandoned toy we ever owned, which the child has dredged up out of the toy chest in his search for his nucleus. Apparently he had to dig pretty deep for that golf ball. Meanwhile, the kitchen is decked out wall-to-wall with facsimiles of mitochondria and ribosomes and vacuoles and strands of glue and little bits of foam, and in the middle of it all sits My List—the neatly organized blueprint of what my day was *supposed* to look like—not a thing checked off, everything pushed forward again, and I think, I will never be caught up, never, never, never.

Plan B:
The Scriptures

TIME MANAGEMENT TURNED out to be more a guilt-producer than a balance-creator for me, so I had to keep looking for the magic formula that would bring balance to my life at last. Around this time, I attended a Relief Society meeting or a Sunday School class or some such event in which I heard the words, "The answers to all of our questions lie in the scriptures." That was certainly not a new thought, but it hit me with particular force on that day. I quickly seized my Triple Combination and turned to the index, eager to be enlightened on the subject of balance. Do you know that the word *balance* does not even appear in the index to the Triple Combination? I found it later in the Topical Guide in my Bible, but even then it referred only to weights and measures. I concluded sadly that Old Testament women must not have had the problems that plague us today, and my answer was not to be found in the scriptures.

It was close to Easter then, and we like to watch the classic movie *The Ten Commandments* with our family around Easter time. (Mostly, I like to watch Yul Brynner, who is about as attractive and magnetic as I can imagine a bald guy being, and Charlton Heston, who is cute even in a long pigtail.) There's a scene in the movie—do you remember it?—where Pharaoh is mad because Moses (Charlton Heston) doesn't come to his birthday party, and Ramses (Yul Brynner) decides to try to get his rival in trouble by charioting down personally with Pharaoh so they can see firsthand what is going on. Moses is overseeing the building of a great city, and his worksite overlooks this immense valley filled with thousands of Hebrew slaves. On the table is one of those scales with the two pans, the type held up by the blindfolded woman in front of courthouses to represent Justice. Ramses begins using the scale as a tool to illustrate the gravity of his accusations against Moses.

"He feeds the slaves with the temple grain," Ramses says, plinking down a little weight on one side of the scale. "He gives them one day in seven to rest." Another weight, another "plink," and the scale tips further to that side. It goes on like this for a while, and Moses just watches. When Ramses is finished making his accusations, Moses picks up a brick from the table and says: "A city is made of bricks. The strong make many; the weak make few; the dead make none." And then he drops that brick on the other side of the scale, and all the little weights of Ramses' accusations go flying. There's no way they can compete.

~

In that moment it came to me in a flash: I don't want *balance.* What I want is the *brick!* I want to find the one thing in my life that, if I get that right, it doesn't matter what the world throws onto the other side of the scale. It won't make any difference at all.

Now, miraculously, all of a sudden the scrip-tures are full of answers. Here are just a few:

Matthew 6:33: "Seek ye first the kingdom of God, and his righteousness; and all these things

> *I don't want* **balance.** *What I want is the* **brick!** *I want to find the one thing in my life that, if I get that right, it doesn't matter what the world throws onto the other side of the scale.*

shall be added unto you." (Get the brick in place first, and everything else will sort itself out.)

Moroni 10:32: "Love God with all your might, mind and strength, then is his grace sufficient for you, that by his grace ye may be perfect in Christ."

And my favorite, in Romans, chapter 8, starting with verse 35, because I can almost hear the little *plinks* on the one side of the scale as Paul is going down his list: "Who shall separate us from the love of Christ? shall tribulation [plink], or distress [plink], or persecution, or famine, or nakedness, or peril, or sword? [plink, plink, plink, plink, plink] . . . Nay, in all these things we are more than conquerors through him that loved us."

The love of Christ, the love of God—their love for us, and our love for them—that love is the brick, and when the brick is in place, everything else works out all right. This, of course, raises the $64,000 question: How do we get the brick in place?

Finding
the Brick

I HAVE OFTEN FELT, as I'm sure you have, the longing in my heart that says, "I'll go where you want me to go, dear Lord." Often I find myself appending to that declaration, "but *where* do you want me to go, dear Lord?" I want to do his will, to show my love for him, but I'm not always certain what that means for me.

What if I supposed, just for a moment, that where I am is exactly where he wants me to be right now? What would it look like if I threw my heart into my mothering, my role as a wife, my work as an employee, with the same fervor my missionary son invests in his proselytizing work?

Let me give you a practical example of how that works in my own life. I have been married for 28 years, so I estimate that I have said about 112 times (figuring it happens roughly once a quarter), "Heavenly Father *told* me to marry you! And I don't think he was mad at me at the time." I don't say this out loud, mind you. But it does cross my thoughts from time to time.

This is partly because I insisted on marrying someone of the opposite gender and partly because my husband grew up in a different family from my own, and those two differences alone have made for some pretty interesting miscommunications.

One assumption I learned I needed to let go of was the way I gauged my husband's love for me on his ability to read my mind. I blame romantic movies for this, at least in part. Have you seen the movie *Only You?* It's about a girl who is convinced her soul mate is a man with a certain name that she heard from a fortune teller. She flies to Italy to find him, and another guy falls in love with her, but sees that she is determined to play this soul-mate thing out. So he agrees to help her find the man. They track him down at a hotel, and she sets up a date, and the guy who loves her (her true soul

One assumption I learned I needed to let go of was the way I gauged my husband's love for me on his ability to read my mind.

mate) buys her a gift for the date. It's a pair of shoes. They are the right size. They are the right color. They are the right style. They are exactly the perfect shoes for the outfit she is planning to wear. Cinderella herself could not have possessed a more ideal shoe.

What man in the world can do this?

This is why those movies are so popular, by the way—because we all want to believe there is someone out there who could discern our every need, sometimes fulfilling needs we didn't even know we had. And so we fall into the trap of "If I have to ask, it doesn't count."

We all want to believe there is someone out there who could discern our every need. And so we fall into the trap of "If I have to ask, it doesn't count."

The sort of ridiculous behavior that this translates to in real life is, for example, me stacking up empty soup cans and cereal boxes until they perch precariously two or three feet above the brim of the kitchen waste can, waiting for my husband to take it out to the trash. Because, you see, if he really loved me, he'd do it without having to be asked.

After nearly three decades of marriage, I have learned that my husband would do just about anything for me. He runs hard and fast, like a train on a track, and the only problem is that if the track doesn't happen to go past the garbage can, he genuinely doesn't see the trash piling up. Now I say, "Honey, could you please take out the garbage?" and he says, "Sure," and he does it. It's a miracle!

The place where all this really breaks down in our household is in the giving of gifts. My husband is one of ten children, and in his growing-up years, a gift-giving occasion such as Christmas or a birthday meant a chance for you to get something you'd had your eye on all year. If you could go to the store with Mom and Dad to pick it out personally, so much the better.

By contrast, I grew up in a family of four children, and my mother was the kind of person who kept track of things in a little notebook. If you admired something in a store in July, it would likely be under the tree for you in December. So Christmas was always a time of wonderful surprises, and I loved being surprised.

I imagined that, after I was married, my husband would demonstrate his intimate understanding of and love for me by the gifts he chose.

I imagined that, after I was married, my husband would demonstrate his intimate understanding of and love for me by the gifts he chose. This was my soul mate, after all, the one I had chosen to spend eternity with. He, more than anyone, would be able to plumb the depths of my heart. I could hardly wait to see what he would choose for me—and I could hardly wait for him to see what I would get for him.

When my husband found out that I intended to surprise him with a Christmas present, he was horrified. The thought that I might spend money from our limited resources on something he might not actually want threw him into a panic. Even worse was the dawning realization that I also expected to be surprised. The expectations imposed by this belief system were so overwhelming that we had more than one fairly miserable Christmas.

Finally, after several years of hissing, we achieved an accommodation that serves us to this day. The rule is (and we have this in a contract), he may pick out his own Christmas present, but he may not have it until Christmas. The latter clause had to be added after he began ordering things in October. And he has to submit to being surprised with one small item, valued at $20 or less, to fulfill my need to surprise someone. On the other end of the deal, I will go with him to pick out my main Christmas present, but then he has to surprise me with something in the $20 range just to prove that he's *trying* to be my soul mate. This compromise works for both of us.

In one of the uneasy years before we reached this agreement, it was getting close to Mother's Day, and my husband came to me early in the week and said, "Honey, they've just called me out of town for work and I won't be back until late Saturday night. I'm going to have to get your Mother's Day present while I'm gone. Please, please, can't you just tell me what to get?"

I had to think about this for a minute. He was going to Elko. I had not ever envisioned Elko as the shopping capital of Nevada, but surely there would be something there that would suit. Then it dawned on me: silver country! Of course!

So I said, "I could really use a pair of silver earrings." His face brightened, and I thought, *I have made it so easy for this man. He won't even have to set foot outside the hotel; he can get a pair of earrings in the gift shop.* This was great: I would get a nice gift, and he would still have to do a little picking out, so it would be really personal as well.

That Saturday night when he returned home, it was clear from the look on his face that he had fulfilled his mission. You know how you feel when you've got just the right present for someone, and you can hardly wait to give it to the person? That's how he looked. So I was pretty excited for the next morning.

Sunday dawned, and the kids came in with the traditional breakfast in bed—soggy Cheerios and slightly burnt toast. Burnt toast is actually fairly symbolic of motherhood, as far as I'm concerned. If you're the one who burned the toast, you scrape it off and eat it yourself so the kids won't have to.

If they burned it, you eat it because they burned it specially for you. However you look at it, you're going to end up consuming a fair amount of burnt toast—and loving it.

So we had the breakfast, and then it was time for the gift. Out came the little package, and the excitement was just dancing in my husband's eyes. I unwrapped the box and opened it carefully. Inside were two pairs of sterling silver earrings.

In the shape of—dinosaurs.

To give credit to my husband's fashion sense, the pairs were actually quite different. There

Burnt toast is actually fairly symbolic of motherhood. If you're the one who burned the toast, you scrape it off and eat it yourself. If they burned it, you eat it because they burned it specially for you.

were little brontosauruses in a kind of flat, hammered, two-dimensional treatment, and little stegosauruses that were three-dimensional and, well, spiky. I looked at those earrings, and then I looked up at my family, and I said, "Thank you!" My husband was grinning from here to Tuesday, and he said, "I thought the kids would get a kick out of those!" What I thought, though I didn't say it out loud, was, *Yes, well, I don't normally put on sterling silver earrings for the kids, sweetheart. I was sort of thinking church, the symphony, a nice occasion.* But he was so happy, and the kids really were getting a kick out of the earrings, that I decided that if nothing else I could be the hit of the preschool carpool.

Do a freeze-frame here and let's take a moment to think about this little incident. Picture that scale again, and put those silly little stegosauruses on one side of it. Now, on the other side, put a husband who honors his priesthood, who loves and serves the Lord, who works every day at a stressful and demanding job so that I can be home taking care of our kids, who loves me enough to want to buy me a Mother's Day present, and who values my role as a mother so much that, when he's picking a gift for me, he believes the thing that will please me most is something that the kids will get a kick out of. Put all those things on the other side of the scale, and you tell me, Do you think the brick is in place? Do you think, in fact, that this might be my soul mate after all?

When we choose to focus on the good, it becomes much easier to see each other as I believe our Father in Heaven sees us.

What I've learned is that part of "I'll go where you want me to go" is "I'll see what you want me to see." In most relationships, there's a whole lot of good along with a pretty stiff dose of not-so-good. When we choose to focus on the good, it becomes much easier to see each other as I believe our Father in Heaven sees us. And that's a lot happier way to live.

The great thing about seeing the world and each other this way is that it doesn't take any more time. It doesn't take an ounce more energy. You don't have to engage more personal resources. You just have to focus in a different way.

Changing
Your Focus

I LEARNED A LITTLE TRICK years ago that helps me make a quick perspective shift when I need to. Our company was participating in a management seminar in which we were taught a strategy that goes by the unlovely name of "reverse your buts." I did not make this up! It works like this:

Maybe you're thinking, "I love you, but you're driving me crazy." Instead, try thinking, "You're driving me crazy, but I love you." Isn't it amazing how different that feels?

Try another one: "I have a great job, but it's really stressful." In reverse, "It's really stressful, but I have a great job."

"I want to serve the Lord, but this calling seems overwhelming." How different does it feel to say, "This calling seems overwhelming, but I want to serve the Lord."

Why does this work? It all goes back to the idea of focus. It's like when my husband made a video recording of our ward's road show years ago. He started with a wide shot, trying to show the whole stage, and then panned across the line of performers and stopped to zoom in for a close up on our own kids. We stop and focus when we get to the thing that is of greatest importance to us. So when you put the

Maybe you're thinking, "I love you, but you're driving me crazy." Instead, try thinking, "You're driving me crazy, but I love you." Isn't it amazing how different that feels?

positive thing last in the sentence, the focus is entirely different.

Again, that's how I think the Lord sees us. He gets the whole picture, good and bad, but he chooses to focus on the good. That is how his love works. That is the brick.

So often we overlook the Lord's tolerance and his capacity to love us when we think of coming unto him. Have you ever thought just what you would do if you knew the Savior was coming to your house tomorrow? Most of us would rush home and clean!

I believe I do that figuratively whenever I think about trying to repent. I think, "I'll just clean up a little first. I'll try to get my act together, and then when I'm ready, I'll be worthy to draw closer to the Lord."

Who do I think I'm kidding? He knows!

He knows I bought the two-pound bag of peanut M&Ms at the store and hid it in my bottom nightstand drawer so I could eat every piece of that candy myself and not have to share with the kids.

He knows the snide remark I made about my coworker two minutes after I promised myself I was going to stop behaving like that.

He knows I had a fight with my teenage daughter that sent her stomping off into her bedroom and left me mad enough to throw something at her locked door—and he knows the fight was largely my fault.

He knows! And he loves me anyway.

If you don't absorb another thing from this whole book, will you make a space in your heart to believe me when I say that he knows, and he loves you anyway. Whatever it is in your life that is separating you from Jesus Christ, he knows about it. He longs for you to come to him *now,* so he can lend you his strength to overcome your weaknesses. His love is there for you, as solid and sturdy as a brick. He doesn't turn away in disgust when you make a mistake, no matter how many times you've made that mistake before. If you'll let him, he'll pick you up and dust you off and say, "Try again. I know you'll do better next time." And because he never gives up on you, you *will* try again, and eventually, with his help, you'll conquer whatever it was that brought you down.

I had an experience once that served as an example of how this works in our lives. I was attending a Suzuki flute recital with my daughter. We weren't participating, just observing, but

Will you make a space in your heart to believe me when I say that he loves you anyway. Whatever it is in your life that is separating you from Jesus Christ, he knows about it.

I could feel the tension in the room in both the performers and their parents, who were watching with that peculiar mixture of pride and terror that we all feel when our loved ones are in the spotlight. If you're familiar with the Suzuki method, you know that everyone works through the same books and learns the same pieces by heart, so all of the lower-level melodies are familiar to the crowd—sometimes painfully so.

One little girl (I'll call her Annie) stood up with a piccolo and announced the name of the march she was planning to play. She began just fine, but when she got to a certain point she lost the thread of the piece and started to fumble around. She looked anxiously at her mother in the audience, and her mom mouthed the words, "Start over," and smiled encouragingly. Annie took a deep breath, and the accompanist went back to the beginning, and off they went—to the same spot, the same mistake, the same loss. This time, Annie gave it all up and ran to her mother, sobbing into her lap.

Some mothers might feel that there was a reputation at stake here. Some might have scolded their child for embarrassing them or wasting the money they had spent on lessons or not being diligent enough in practicing. But Annie's mother wasn't like that. She patted her daughter's back and took her outside and dried her tears and brought her back in to hear the rest of the performers, none of whom messed up in any noticeable way. I remember thinking she probably wanted Annie to see what was possible for her. I thought it was great, really.

Then, at the end of the recital, something happened that took my breath away. The hostess of the event stood up and thanked all the participants and then said, with a smile on her face, "Annie would like to try her piece again."

Any tension that may have been in the room before was nothing compared to the feeling at that moment. Every person there was literally leaning forward in his or her chair, straining to telegraph support to a little girl with a piccolo. It had been decided that Annie should try the piece using the music, so that she could recover if she lost her place. The accompanist began playing, and we all held our breaths as Annie rounded the corner into the problem spot. After a little quaver, she pushed right on through to the end. Again she turned and ran to her mother, but this time it was with a look of pure joy. She had done it!

That is precisely how I like to picture the Lord's loving care for us. We have had many lessons, we have studied and practiced and prepared carefully, and still we mess up sometimes. When that happens, he doesn't give us some big lecture on how we've let him down. He doesn't ask us how on earth we could have made that mistake when we *know* better. Instead, he takes us out and calms us down and gives us another chance, maybe with a little extra help. He knows we didn't perform to capacity, but he clearly believes that we will, someday. Meanwhile, his loving acceptance of what we *were* able to give helps us have the confidence to keep trying, to keep improving, to not give up on ourselves.

A Formula for Feeling God's Love

THERE IS A WAY TO FEEL the Lord's love more fully in your life. The simple, three-step formula comes from Doctrine and Covenants, section 90, verse 24:

1. Search diligently.

Have you ever searched for something without knowing what it was you were searching for? It would be kind of silly, wouldn't it, wandering around the house, looking under couch cushions and behind chairs. "What are you doing, Mom?" "Searching. Just searching."

That's not how it works, of course. When you're searching, it helps to have the object of the search in mind. And yet we sometimes "search" the scriptures without having in mind what it is we're looking for. May I suggest the more productive approach of searching diligently by choosing something to be watching for? And if you don't know what to look for, may I suggest that you search for the brick. Look for evidences of God's love for you—I promise they are everywhere in the scriptures. You can also look for ways to show your love for him. Those, too, are abundant in the examples of scriptural figures.

2. Pray always.

I love the injunction to pray always. I'm afraid that if the scripture said, "Pray for 45 minutes every morning before you start your day," I would never measure up. Although I can testify of the importance and worth of finding solitary time and space for personal prayer, the practical fact of the matter is that time and space are not always readily available. However, the phrase "pray always" suggests to me that I can pray any-time, anywhere—and I do. I pray in my car. I pray on my way to a meeting. I pray as I'm waving my child off to school. And when I can, I lock my door and pray on my knees, but if I waited to pray every time until those condi-tions were just right, I wouldn't be able to say nearly as many prayers as I need to.

Again, if you're won-dering what to pray for, may I suggest that you pray to feel God's love for you. He will manifest it to you in marvelous ways if you will ask, seek,

The phrase "pray always" suggests to me that I can pray anytime, anywhere —and I do. I pray in my car. I pray on my way to a meeting. And when I can, I lock my door and pray on my knees.

and knock as he has so generously invited us to do.

3. Be believing.

Believe that your search is not in vain. Believe that you will find what you're looking for. Believe that the brick is there for you personally—not just as some abstract concept but as the most intimate, knowledge-filled, careful love you could ever know. Believe that if the Lord spoke to you today he would call you by name. He knows you that well.

That's the formula: "Search diligently, pray always, and be believing." And here's Heavenly Father's part of the covenant: "And all things shall work together for your good, if ye walk uprightly" (D&C 90:24). Can you feel the tremendous power of that promise? *All* things. Not just the good things. Not just the happy things. Not just the birthdays and the missionary calls and the promotions and the straight-A report cards and the sunshine-on-parade-day things. *All* things can work for our good. That's a pretty solid brick to have in place!

One of the most meaningful examples of this principle that I've ever heard of is in the story of a little pioneer girl named Agnes Caldwell. Before I share it, let me just say that I love pioneer stories. I always feel the awe of what those people went through so that the gospel could survive on the earth at a time when Satan seemed so determined and so nearly able to crush it.

I was interested to read recently that many companies of handcart pioneers made their way across the plains safely. Handcart migration was a viable option for quite some time, in fact. We hear very little about the companies who made it without incident to the Salt Lake Valley, although I think their trek must still have been arduous. But the ones we hear about, the ones we talk about and remember and revere for their sacrifice, are the Willie and Martin handcart companies, the ones that almost entirely perished on the plains.

I have a theory about the Willie and Martin handcart pioneers. I believe the Lord allowed a select group of people to lay everything they had on the altar so that we could understand the existence of that kind of faith.

Here are some questions that always come to my mind when I think of those Willie and Martin pioneers: Why didn't the Lord stop them? Why did he let them start out so late in the year? Or, at the very least, why didn't he temper the elements, holding back the winter instead of allowing the snow to come so early to Wyoming that year?

I don't know the answers to those questions, but I have a theory about the sacrifices made by the Willie and Martin handcart pioneers. I believe those sacrifices might have been made for us. I believe the Lord allowed a select group of people to lay everything they had on the altar so that we who came after them could understand in some small measure the existence of that kind of faith. I believe he accepted and sanctified their actions in such a way that generations to come would find the courage to keep putting one foot in front of the other, as they did.

Agnes Caldwell and her family traveled with the Willie company and suffered terrible hardships with the others. When the rescue wagons came, they took on all the infirm and those who could walk no farther, but the able-bodied still had to press forward on foot. Nine-year-old Agnes and some of the other children decided to try to keep up with the wagons in hopes of being offered a ride. Sure enough, after a time one of the drivers asked her if she'd like to ride with him, an invitation she gratefully accepted. As she tells the story:

"At this he reached over, taking my hand, clucking to his horses to make me run, with legs that seemed to me could run no farther. On we went, to what to me seemed miles. What went through my head at that time was that he was the meanest man that ever lived or that I had ever heard of."

I've tried to imagine this scene. I've pictured a little girl who had given everything she knew how to give for a cause she had been taught was dearer than life itself. I've wondered how it must have felt to finally be offered some relief and then have it just as suddenly withdrawn.

Agnes continues: "Just at what seemed the breaking point, he stopped. Taking a blanket, he wrapped me up and lay me in the bottom of the wagon, warm and comfortable. Here I had time to change my mind, as I surely did, knowing full well by doing this he saved me from freezing when taken into the wagon" (Susan Arrington Madsen, "Handcart Girl," *Friend,* October 1997, 35).

I have thought of this story many times when I find myself or my friends in what I would call "running-beside-the-wagon" moments. I have wondered if, at such times, when we have given all we have to give, relying on the promise that the Lord will lift us up, when we are questioning why he doesn't pull us into the wagon, when we are about to collapse from the sheer exhaustion of it all—what if we stopped and listened to the Spirit? Perhaps we might hear him saying, "Wait. Wait just a little longer. You don't know what I'm trying to save here." Maybe the message would even be, "You don't know *who* I'm trying to save here. You don't know whose life might be eternally affected by your willingness to hang on for one more moment, to keep taking step after step. I promise I won't leave you to drop. I know what you can bear, and your trials will not exceed your capacity." I have to trust that the Lord knows what he is doing with my life, even in those hard moments when I can't possibly see what he has in mind.

Beauty
for Ashes

*A*LL THINGS SHALL WORK together for your good. Do you believe it? Have you really thought about his wonderful promise, given through the prophet Isaiah, that he will give you "beauty for ashes"? (See Isaiah 61:3.) Ponder that one for a minute. Think about ashes, about what is left over after the most horrific destruction has occurred. Then picture the Lord taking that devastation and turning it into something beautiful. That is the sure promise of the Atonement: that all our losses will be made up to us. When a brick such as that is in place, nothing that can happen in mortality could ever shake us.

But we have to stick with it. We have to keep moving forward until we claim the blessings the Lord means for us to have. We must do this even when the way is not clear to us. I remember a time when I attended a conference at Brigham Young University and ended up staying late for several extra events. By the time I finished all my visiting and enjoying the people I met, it was nearly 10:30 P.M. I hurried up to where I had left my car, and found the parking lot quite deserted except for my vehicle. I was nervous, emotionally tired from a long day, and physically worn out from the brisk walk in the dark. With a sigh of relief I dropped into the front seat of the car, started it up, and headed for the exit.

There was just one problem—it wasn't the exit. It was the entrance, and there was no way out in that direction. I immediately began looking around for the exit, but it was nowhere in sight. This was ridiculous! There were no other

cars in the lot to impede my view. I just didn't
know which way to go.

Ultimately it occurred to me that the arrows
painted on the asphalt were there for a reason. I
decided they would lead me to the exit if I fol-
lowed them. I'm sure this makes perfect sense in
the middle of the day, when the parking lot is
crowded and the traffic flow needs to be man-
aged. I have to tell you, I felt a little stupid weav-
ing around that parking lot in the dead of night
to follow those arrows. I'm sure I must have
passed the same tree three or four times until
finally, finally, there was an exit in sight up ahead.
And the gate was *closed.*

By now I was practically beside myself. I
checked carefully for a call box or a button or
something that I could push to release the gate
or summon help, but there was nothing. Oh, I
was frustrated! I was grumbling to myself, *This is
just great! BYU has these curfew rules, and everybody in the*

world but me knows enough to get their cars out of the parking lot before 10:00, and now I'm going to have to call my husband and have him drive all the way down to Provo to pick me up, and then we'll have to get up early in the morning and drive all the way down again to get my car. . . . The whole time I was fretting about this, I kept rolling slowly closer and closer to the gate, and all of a sudden it popped up all by itself! Automatic gate! Who knew?

Since that night, I have wondered how many times I may have missed out on a blessing because I assumed the way was closed to me, when if I had just kept going, kept trying, kept moving forward, a path would have been opened, even miraculously so. We have to hang in there. We have to stay the course, and when we do so, the blessings await us not just at the journey's end but all along the way.

Here, then, is why I am still an unbalanced woman: because I have learned there is something better than balance—something more desirable and more attainable and infinitely more practical. It is the brick, the love of God, and I want to do whatever I can to feel that love. To that end—

- I'll see what he wants me to see,

- I'll focus on the good things in my life instead of the imperfections,

- I'll accept his love and his infinite patience and his help with my strivings to do better,

- I'll search diligently, pray always, and be believing that his charity applies to me personally,

I have wondered how many times I may have missed out on a blessing because I assumed the way was closed to me, when if I had just kept going, a path would have been opened.

• I'll trust that he knows how the pieces of my life will all fit together to work for my good, and

• I'll keep going forward, one step at a time, until I claim the blessings he means for me to have.

When I do these things, I can feel that the brick is in place. I can feel the Lord's love for me, and it fills me in turn with a tremendous love for him and for all his children. I testify to you of the truth of this love and of the power it can give you to carry on, and I do so in the name of the one who bestows it, even Jesus Christ.